Sis the Cat

A Division of The McGraw·Hill Companies

Columbus, Ohio

www.sra4kids.com

SRA/McGraw-Hill

A Division of The McGraw·Hill Companies

Printed in the United States of America.

Send all inquiries to:
SRA/McGraw-Hill
8787 Orion Place
Columbus, OH 43240-4027

ISBN 0-07-569435-2
3 4 5 6 7 8 9 DBH 05 04 03 02

Sis and Dad

There is Sis. Sis spins and stops on the mat.

Sis can sit.
Sis can nap.

Sis can bat.
Sis can tap.

Sis bats the pans.
Sis hits the hat.

Dad is mad.
Bad cat!

Where Is Sis?

Sis scats.
Where is Sis?

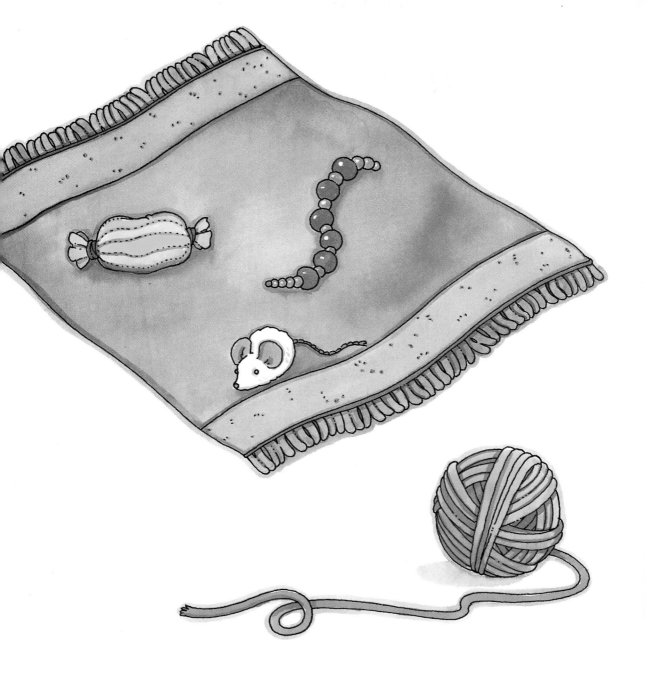

Is Sis on the mat?
Sis is not on the mat.

Is Sis in the hat?
Sis is not in the hat.

Is Sis in a tin pan?
Sis is not in a tin pan.

Is Sis with Pam and Bob?
No, Sis is not with Pam and Bob.

I miss Sis.
Where is Sis?

Dad has Sis.
Sis sits on him.

Dad is not mad.
And Sis is not sad.

I can sit with Sis and Dad.